PRO SPORTS CHAMPIONSHIPS
ROSE BOWL

Lauren Diemer

AV² provides enriched content that supplements and complements this book. Weigl's AV² books strive to create inspired learning and engage young minds in a total learning experience.

Your AV² Media Enhanced books come alive with...

 Audio
Listen to sections of the book read aloud.

 Key Words
Study vocabulary, and complete a matching word activity.

 Video
Watch informative video clips.

 Quizzes
Test your knowledge.

Go to www.av2books.com, and enter this book's unique code.

Embedded Weblinks
Gain additional information for research.

Slide Show
View images and captions, and prepare a presentation.

BOOK CODE

Q479959

Try This!
Complete activities and hands-on experiments.

...and much, much more!

AV² by Weigl brings you media enhanced books that support active learning.

Published by AV² by Weigl
350 5th Avenue, 59th Floor
New York, NY 10118
Website: www.av2books.com   www.weigl.com

Library of Congress Cataloging-in-Publication Data
Diemer, Lauren.
Rose Bowl / Lauren Diemer.
    p. cm.– (Pro sports championships)
Includes index.
Summary: "Provides information about the Rose Bowl championship, including analysis of the sport, an outline of its rules, and information about the location where the competition takes place. Intended for a fourth to sixth grade audience"—Provided by publisher.
ISBN 978-1-62127-367-7 (hardcover : alk. paper) — ISBN 978-1-62127-372-1 (softcover : alk. paper)
1. Rose Bowl (Football game)—History—Juvenile literature. I. Title.
GV957.R6D54 2013
796.3326309794'93—dc23
                         2012043080

Printed in the United States of America in North Mankato, Minnesota
1 2 3 4 5 6 7 8 9 0 17 16 15 14 13

012013
WEP301112

PROJECT COORDINATOR Aaron Carr   EDITOR Steve Macleod   ART DIRECTOR Terry Paulhus

Every reasonable effort has been made to trace ownership and to obtain permission to reprint copyright material. The publishers would be pleased to have any errors or omissions brought to their attention so that they may be corrected in subsequent printings.

Weigl acknowledges Getty Images as the primary image supplier for this book.

CONTENTS

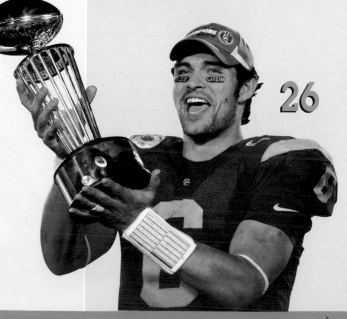

What is the Rose Bowl?

The Rose Bowl is a championship football game. It is played between two of the best college football teams in the United States. The game is played in Pasadena, California, on New Year's Day. If New Year's Day falls on a Sunday, the game is played on January 2.

The Rose Bowl was created as part of the Tournament of Roses. This tournament is also known as "America's New Year Celebration." It is a festival of flowers, music, and sporting events. It began on New Year's Day in 1890. The Rose Bowl was first played during the Tournament of Roses in 1902. After that first game, there was not another Rose Bowl game for 14 years. The Rose Bowl has been played every year since 1916.

University of Wisconsin quarterback Russell Wilson had 296 yards passing and two touchdowns in the 2012 Rose Bowl. Wisconsin lost the game 45–38 to Oregon.

The Rose Bowl has been one of the most popular college football games since 1945. It has become one of the highest-attended sporting events in the country. The Rose Bowl has been sold out each year since 1947.

The Rose Bowl is the oldest **bowl game** in the United States. It has gained the nickname, "The Granddaddy of Them All."

CHANGES THROUGHOUT THE YEARS	
PAST	**PRESENT**
California and Washington & Jefferson tie 0–0 in the Rose Bowl. California completes zero passes and has 49 yards rushing.	USC defeats Illinois 49–17 in the Rose Bowl. USC sets a Rose Bowl record with 633 offensive yards and ties the bowl game record for most points with 49.
The Rose Bowl was played at Pasadena's Tournament Park in 1916 in front of 7,000 fans.	The Rose Bowl is played at the Rose Bowl Stadium in 2012 in front of 91,245 fans.
Only one bowl game was played annually in the 1930s.	In 2012, 35 National Collegiate Athletic Association (NCAA) bowl games were played.

Rose Bowl Trophies

The Rose Bowl winner earns the Leishman Trophy. It is named after William L. Leishman. He was the president of the 1920 Tournament of Roses. He was responsible for building the Rose Bowl Stadium. The trophy is made from about 16 pounds (7.3 kilograms) of silver. It is almost 21 inches (53 centimeters) tall. The Most Valuable Player (MVP) in each Rose Bowl receives a crystal trophy. This award was created in 1953. It was given **retroactively** to 1902. Starting in 2005, a **defensive** and an **offensive** player were named MVP for each Rose Bowl.

Rose Bowl History

Football was becoming a popular sport in the early 1900s. Organizers of the Tournament of Roses thought hosting a major football event would be a great way to start the New Year. The Rose Bowl was originally titled the Tournament East-West Football Game.

The first game was played in 1902. It was between the University of Michigan and Stanford University. Michigan's football team had been the best team in the country that season. The team had won all 10 of the games it had played. The event organizers thought a big crowd would come out to watch the team play.

The Michigan Wolverines have won seven national championships and 42 **conference** championships.

The Rose Bowl became the first college football game to be broadcast nationally in color and the first to broadcast live to many parts of the world. People across the country watch the game on television today.

The Rose Bowl has a halftime show between the second and third quarters. This usually involves live music and performances.

Stanford had a strong team as well, but they were no match for Michigan. Stanford stopped playing in the third quarter. Michigan won the game with a score of 49–0.

The Tournament of Roses organizers hoped the game would be more exciting. They decided to focus on different events for the next 14 years. They held chariot races, ostrich races, and a race between a camel and an elephant.

Another football game was planned for the 1916 Tournament of Roses. Washington State defeated Brown University that year. The Rose Bowl has been played every year since.

Rose Bowl Royalty

About 1,000 young women apply to become the Rose Bowl Queen each year. Finalists are judged on their poise, school achievements, public speaking skills, and personalities. The winner is chosen after one month of interviews. Six runners up are named princesses. The queen and princesses ride on the Royal Court float in the Rose Bowl Parade. They also attend events during the year to promote the Tournament of Roses.

Rules of the Game

Football has many rules. They have been changed over the years. A number of rules have been created to keep players safe from injury.

1 Playing the Game

The goal of a football game is to carry the ball into the opposing team's end zone. Teams can run with the ball or pass the ball. The offense has four downs, or chances, to move the ball 10 yards down the field. If the ball is moved 10 yards or more, the offense starts again at first down. They have four more chances to move the ball at least another 10 yards. The defense tries to stop the offense from moving the ball ahead.

2 Line of Scrimmage

The line of scrimmage is where the two teams meet at the beginning of the play. At least seven offensive players face the defending team on the line before the **snap**. Defending players are positioned to block the offensive team's players. Players not on the line of scrimmage must be at least one yard behind it.

3 Scoring Points

Points are scored when a team gets a touchdown, field goal, or conversion. A team gets a touchdown when one of its players has possession of the ball in the other team's end zone. A touchdown is worth six points. After a touchdown, the scoring team can earn more points. This is called a conversion. The ball can be kicked through the goalposts for one extra point. The ball can also be taken across the goal line for two points. Conversion plays begin two yards from the end zone. A field goal is scored when a kicker sends the ball through the goalposts. It is worth three points.

4 Offside

If a defensive player moves across the line of scrimmage before the ball is snapped, they are offside. If the player does not move back to their side of the line before the play starts a penalty is given. The offense moves 5 yards up the field.

5 On the Clock

There are four quarters in a game of football. Each quarter is 15 minutes. It takes about three hours to play all four quarters. This is because the clock stops during the game. The game clock is stopped at different times, such as when a player goes out of bounds, when there is an incomplete pass, when there is a penalty, and when a team scores.

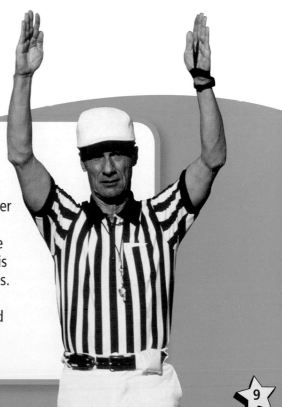

Making the Call

Referees wear black and white striped shirts. They make sure the players follow the rules of the game. Referees determine if a player has scored a touchdown, gone out of bounds, or committed a **foul**. The referee throws a flag on the field if he or she sees a rule being broken. The referee then hands out a penalty. One referee is responsible for the game. He is assisted by up to six other referees. These referees have specific jobs. A line judge watches to see if the ball goes out of bounds and determines where the ball should be placed when play starts. Other judges include the side judge, the back judge, the game judge, and the umpire.

The Football Field

Football is played on a rectangular field. It is 100 yards (91.4 meters) long and 160 feet (48.8 m) wide. At each end of the field, there is a section that measures 10 yards long. This is called the end zone. Lines that run across the field parallel to the goal line are called yard lines. They are labeled every 10 yards from 10 to 50 on each side of the field. The 50-yard line is also called midfield. Yard lines help measure how far the football has moved from the line of scrimmage.

Hash marks are two sets of short lines that run down the left and right side of the field. They mark single yards. They help show where the ball should be placed at the start of a play. Each play in football starts between or on the hash marks.

Major renovation plans were made for Rose Bowl Stadium in 2009. They will be complete for the 100th Rose Bowl game in 2014.

The line that separates the main field from the end zone is called the goal line. Goalposts are positioned on the back line of each end zone.

The field can be made up of real grass or artificial **turf**. Real grass does not last as long under the wear and tear of the game. Some stadiums are indoors, so grass is harder to grow. Turf is used instead of grass in these stadiums.

Players on the Team

A football team has 11 offensive and defensive players on the field at one time. The offense consists of the quarterback, linesmen, backs, tight ends, and receivers. The defense is made up of linesman, linebackers, cornerbacks, and safeties. The quarterback takes the ball at the snap, decides plays, and passes the ball to receivers or running backs. Running backs run with the ball to gain yards. Wide receivers catch passes. The center, offensive guards, and offensive tackles, are blocking positions. They make sure that the quarterback and receivers can move the ball without the other team's defensive players stopping them. Tight ends block on the line of scrimmage and catch passes. Defensive ends stop the quarterback from throwing the ball or running with it. Defensive tackles, nose guards, and linebackers try to keep the offense from gaining yards. Cornerbacks and safeties keep the opposing team from catching passes. Other players on a team include the kicker and **punter**.

THE FOOTBALL FIELD

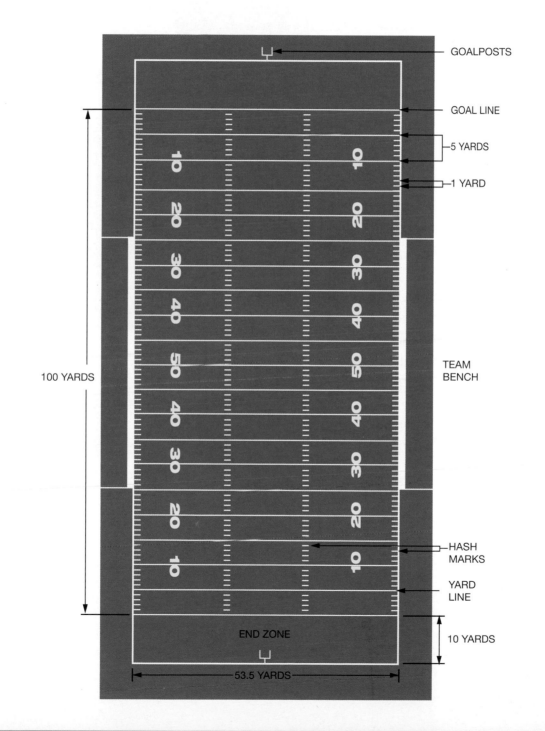

GOALPOSTS

GOAL LINE

5 YARDS

1 YARD

100 YARDS

TEAM BENCH

HASH MARKS

YARD LINE

END ZONE

10 YARDS

53.5 YARDS

11

Football Equipment

Football players run into each other with a great deal of speed. The defense does this to stop the other team from moving down the field and into the end zone. The offense does this so their teammates can move the ball ahead. Special gear is worn to protect the players from injury.

One of the most important pieces of equipment is the helmet. Helmets are made of hard plastic. They are lined with foam and air cushions. This helps soften a hit to the head from other players or from the ground. Helmets also have metal or plastic bars called a facemask. This protects the face.

Helmet

Shoulder pads

Jersey

Gloves

Shorts

Socks

Cleats

Early footballs were made of inflated pig bladders, giving the ball the commonly used name "pigskin." Today, footballs are made of leather surrounding an inflated rubber pouch.

Shoulder pads

Shoulder pads protect the player's shoulders and collarbone. They are made of hard plastic and are lined with foam. Each position wears different shoulder pads. Linebackers have big pads because they hit other players with their shoulders when they try to tackle them. Receivers wear smaller pads so they can run faster and catch the ball more easily.

Thigh, knee, hip, tailbone, rib, and elbow pads help protect the players when they get hit or tackled. Players also wear mouth guards to keep their teeth from being damaged during the game.

Mouth guard

Some players wear special gloves to help them hold onto the football. Most players wear special football shoes called cleats. These shoes help them grip the field and keep players from slipping on the grass or turf. Cleats have flat-tipped spikes on the bottom.

Cleats

Team Uniforms

College football uniforms come in many colors. Teams most often wear the same colors as those used by the university the team represents. This helps **spectators** tell teams apart during a game. The jersey has short sleeves and fits tightly over the shoulder pads. Each player's number is on the front and back, along with the team name or logo. Some teams also put each player's last name on the back of the jersey. Football players wear tight pants. The pants are cut off just below the knee. Players always wear their helmets as part of their uniforms.

Qualifying to Play

Rose Bowl games used to be played between a team from the Pacific Coast Conference (PCC) and a team they invited to the game, typically from the eastern states. Neither team had to be the champions of their conference or state. After 1946, the rules changed slightly. A team from the Pacific Coast Conference, known as the Pac-12 Conference today, played a team from one of the midwestern and eastern universities that made up the Big Ten Conference.

During World War II, many teams had to withdraw from qualifying for the Rose Bowl. Many of their players had stopped attending university to fight in the war instead. Other players took regular jobs to help with the shortage of workers caused by the number of men fighting in the war. Some schools did not have enough players to field a team.

Some colleges continued to play during the war. Special rules were put in place to help teams whose players had gone to war.

During World War II, the army and air force held football games for the men fighting in the war.

The United States entered World War II in 1941. As a result, the Parade of Roses was cancelled in 1942. There was concern a large gathering of people on the west coast would be a target for an attack.

Duke University and Oregon State were scheduled to play in the Rose Bowl in 1942. Instead of canceling the game, Duke invited Oregon to play at its stadium in North Carolina. Oregon State won the game 20–16 in front of a crowd of 56,000 people.

The Rose Bowl became part of the Bowl Championship Series (BCS) in 1998. There are five bowl games played across the United States each year in the BCS to determine the best football teams in the country. There are four major bowl games and one national championship game. The site of each bowl game takes a turn hosting the national championship game. In 2010, Rose Bowl Stadium hosted the Rose Bowl and the national championship game one week later.

Penn State has played in the Rose Bowl three times. They won the bowl game in 1995.

Pac-12 Conference

The Pacific Coast Conference was formed in 1916 with four teams. The conference became the Pacific 8 Conference in 1968, when four more teams joined. It then became the Pacific 10 (Pac-10) in 1978. Two more universities joined the conference in 2011 and it was renamed the Pac-12. The Rose Bowl has been in association with the Big Ten and Pac-12 Conferences since 1946. Often, the champion of the Big Ten Conference plays the champion of the Pac-12 Conference on January 1 in Pasadena each year.

Where They Play

Until 1922, all of the Rose Bowl games were played at California's Tournament Park in Pasadena. In 1920, Pasadena city officials decided the football field at Tournament Park was too small for the growing New Year's Day crowd at the annual football game. Construction on a new horseshoe-shaped stadium was completed in 1922. The new stadium was nicknamed the Rose Bowl. The first Rose Bowl game was played in 1923. The stadium cost $272,198 to build. Seat subscriptions bought by 210 individuals and companies paid for the costs.

When it was first built, the Rose Bowl Stadium held 57,000 people. Today, more than 92,500 people can be seated inside the stadium.

The Rose Bowl Stadium measures 880 feet (268 m) in length from the north to south rims, and 695 feet (212 m) wide from the east to west rims.

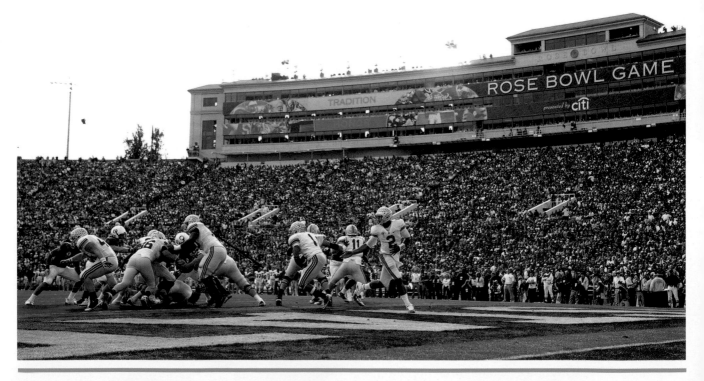

There are more than 100 varieties of rose bushes between the stadium and the fence around it.

The U.S. National Register of Historic Places has named the Rose Bowl Stadium a National Historic Landmark. Though it is known mainly for the New Year's Tournament of Roses football game, five National Football League Super Bowl games have been played there. It is also home to the UCLA Bruins football team. Also, the 1994 FIFA World Cup soccer final, the 1999 Women's World Cup soccer final, 1932 and 1984 Olympic soccer matches, Fourth of July celebrations, concerts, and the world's largest flea market have been hosted at the Rose Bowl Stadium.

It would take about 84,375,000 gallons (319,394,138 liters) of water to fill the Rose Bowl Stadium to the rim.

Rose Bowl Final Scores

YEAR	WINNING TEAM	SCORE	LOSING TEAM	SCORE
2012	Oregon	45	Wisconsin	38
2011	TCU	21	Wisconsin	19
2010	Ohio State	26	Oregon	17
2009	USC	38	Penn State	24
2008	USC	49	Illinois	17
2007	USC	32	Michigan	18
2006	Texas	41	USC	38
2005	Texas	38	Michigan	37
2004	USC	28	Michigan	14
2003	Oklahoma	34	Washington State	14
2002	Miami	37	Nebraska	14

Mapping Rose Bowl Winners

Oregon

2012

Pacific Ocean

Oklahoma

2003

USC

2004, 2007, 2008, 2009

Texas

2005, 2006

UNITED STATES

MEXICO

Many teams have had the honor of playing in the Rose Bowl since the first game in 1902. This map shows the locations of the winning teams from 2002 to 2012.

WINNING TEAMS FROM 2002 TO 2012

Miami: 2002
Oklahoma: 2003
Texas: 2005, 2006
USC: 2004, 2007, 2008, 2009
Ohio State: 2010
TCU: 2011
Oregon: 2012

N
W E
S

Scale | 621 Miles
0 | 1,000 Kilometers

CANADA

Ohio State
2010

TCU
2011

Atlantic
Ocean

Miami
2002

Women in Football

Women's football has a long history in the United States. In 1926, one of the first organized games was played when the Frankford Yellow Jackets hired women to play during halftime at their games. Since that time, there have been many women's football events. There are **semi-professional** and **amateur** leagues all over the country. In some cases, women even play on men's teams.

The Women's Professional Football League (WPFL) was formed in 1965 by a businessman named Sid Friedman. Nine years later, the National Women's Football League (NWFL) was established. The leagues had some success in the beginning, but they did not make enough money to continue operating.

In recent years, several new women's football leagues have started in North America. They include the Independent Women's Football League (IWFL), the Women's Western Canadian Football League, and the Maritime Women's Football League. The Women's Football Alliance (WFA) is a new league that began in 2009. Two years later, a number of teams from other leagues joined the WFA. There are 64 teams in this league.

The Detroit Demolition had a 52-game winning streak between the 2002 and 2006 seasons.

The International Federation of American Football (AFAF) held the first World's Women Championship in 2010. The tournament was played in Sweden. The United States defeated Canada 66-0 in the final game to win the gold medal. Jessica Springer rushed for 161 yards and four touchdowns in the game.

The Detroit Demolition have played in four different leagues. They have won five championship titles.

In addition to professional and semi-professional organizations, girls can play **touch football** and **flag football**. In some of these leagues, boys and girls play on the same teams. Sometimes, girls play tackle football with the boys on their community or high school teams.

Women's Football Leagues

The IWFL began in 2000. About 1,600 women play in this league in both the United States and Canada. The league is made up of 30 teams, and it has a championship game each year. In 2009, the IWFL had a bowl game called the Pink Ribbon Bowl.

Historical Highlights

The Rose Bowl is the college football bowl game with the longest history. It has had many significant historical moments.

The first game played at the Rose Bowl stadium in 1923 was between the University of Southern California (USC) and Pennsylvania State University (Penn State). It was the ninth Rose Bowl, but it was the first appearance at the event for both teams. USC won 14–3. The low-scoring game was not a very exciting way to open the new stadium. The entire last quarter of the game was played without either team scoring a point.

In 1947, UCLA and Illinois University faced off in the Rose Bowl. Illinois beat UCLA by a score of 45–14. During the game, UCLA's Al Hoisch returned a kickoff 103 yards for a touchdown. This is the longest **kick return** in Rose Bowl history.

The 2005 Rose Bowl was the first time a Big Ten champion did not face a team from the Pac-12 since 1947. Michigan University played the University of Texas. Texas kicked the ball through the **uprights** just as the fourth quarter ended. They won the game by a single point. This was the first time these two teams had faced one another, even though both teams had been playing for many years.

Oregon quarterback Danny O'Neil set the record for most passing yards in the Rose Bowl. He threw for 456 yards during the 1995 game.

The University of Texas played in the Rose Bowl again in 2006. That year, its opponents were the USC Trojans. Both teams had very strong regular seasons leading up to the Rose Bowl. Again, the game was close. Vince Young of Texas scored a last-minute touchdown to give USC its first Rose Bowl loss since 1989.

Only four players in Rose Bowl history have been named MVP more than once. Charles White won the award in 1979 and 1980.

ROSE BOWL MVPS 2002 TO 2012		
NAME	**TEAM**	**YEAR**
Lavasier Tuinei (Offense) Kiko Alonso (Defense)	Oregon	2012
Andy Dalton (Offense) Tank Carder (Defense)	TCU	2011
Terrelle Pryor (Offense) Kenny Rowe (Defense)	Ohio State Oregon	2010
Mark Sanchez (Offense) Kaluka Maiava (Defense)	USC	2009
John David Booty (Offense) Rey Maualuga (Defense)	USC	2008
Dwayne Darrett (Offense) Brian Cushing (Defense)	USC	2007
Vince Young (Offense) Michael Huff (Defense)	Texas	2006
Vince Young (Offense) LaMarr Woodley (Defense)	Texas Michigan	2005
Matt Leinart	USC	2004
Nate Hybl	Oklahoma University	2003
Ken Dorsey & Andre Johnson	Miami	2002

LEGENDS
and Current Stars

Andre Johnson – Wide Receiver

Andre Johnson joined the University of Miami in 2000. The football team had 5 wins and 6 losses a few years earlier. In the 2001 season, Miami had 12 wins and no losses. They defeated Nebraska 37–14 in the Rose Bowl. Johnson had 199 yards receiving and two touchdowns during the game. He and Miami quarterback Ken Dorsey won the Rose Bowl MVP award for the game. In 2003, Johnson was drafted by the Houston Texans. He led the NFL in receiving yards in 2008 and 2009. He has played in five NFL Pro Bowls.

Warren Moon

Andre Johnson

Warren Moon – Quarterback

Warren Moon began his college football career playing quarterback for the University of Washington Huskies. He helped the Huskies get to the 1978 Rose Bowl, which they won despite being the **underdog**. Moon was named MVP of that Rose Bowl game. He then went on to play in both the Canadian Football League (CFL) and the National Football League (NFL). Moon set many football records. He was inducted into the Rose Bowl Hall of Fame in 1997.

Dick Butkus

Mark Sanchez – Quarterback

Mark Sanchez joined the USC football team in 2005. He spent his first three seasons as the backup quarterback. As the starting quarterback in 2008, Sanchez had 3,207 yards passing and 34 touchdowns. The team was ranked 5th overall in the country. In the Rose Bowl game that followed that season, Sanchez passed for 413 yards and four touchdowns. USC defeated Penn State 38–24. Sanchez was named the game's MVP. Sanchez was drafted by the New York Jets in the 2009 NFL draft.

Dick Butkus – Linebacker

Dick Butkus played for the University of Illinois from 1962 to 1964. He is considered one of the best players of his generation. Butkus was inducted into the Rose Bowl Hall of Fame in 1995. He is also in the Pro Football Hall of Fame. The Dick Butkus Award is given out each year to the most outstanding linebacker in college football.

Mark Sanchez

Famous Firsts

The Rose Bowl game played on January 1, 1947, was the first "modern day" Rose Bowl game. The 1947 game pitted the champions of the Pac-12 against the champions of the Big Ten.

The first Rose Bowl game played as a Bowl Championship Series (BCS) game was played on January 1, 1999. It was between Wisconsin and UCLA. Wisconsin won the game 38–31.

In 2002, the Rose Bowl was not played between the Pac-12 champion and the Big Ten champion for the first time since 1947. When the Rose Bowl became part of the Bowl Championship Series, the game would be used to determine college football's national champion some years. In 2002, the Miami Hurricanes defeated the Nebraska Cornhuskers to win the BCS.

USC quarterback Mark Sanchez helped his team win the 95th Rose Bowl in 2009.

At the Rose Bowl in 2009, USC became the first team to win three straight Rose Bowls. Led by Mark Sanchez, USC won 38–24 over Penn State. Sanchez, USC's quarterback, set a Rose Bowl **pass completion** record. Eighty percent of the passes he threw were caught by USC players.

USC has won the Rose Bowl more times than any other team. They have won the game 24 times.

Bowl Championship Series

In the early 1990s, the Bowl Coalition formed. It was made up of five conferences, as well as one individual team—Notre Dame. The coalition took part in six bowl games each year, not including the Rose Bowl. Before this time, teams signed contracts to take part in specific bowl games. This meant they could not play in other bowl games. Under the new agreement, teams could play in any of the bowl games if it meant that a clear national champion could be determined. However, many teams, including those contracted to play in the Rose Bowl, were not part of the agreement. This meant that if one of the top-ranked teams was from the Big Ten or Pac-12, it could not take part in a national championship game. The Bowl Championship Series began in 1998, so a clear national champion could be established. The Rose Bowl Association agreed to let its teams take part. The Rose Bowl, the Orange Bowl, the Sugar Bowl, and the Fiesta Bowl take turns hosting the BCS championship game, as well as hosting their own bowl games.

The Rise of the Rose Bowl

1890

The first Tournament of Roses celebration takes place.

1916

The Rose Bowl returns to the Tournament of Roses.

1923

The Rose Bowl game is played in the Rose Bowl Stadium for the first time.

1900

The first East–West football game, is played at the Tournament of Roses.

1902

The first Rose Bowl game is played. It is not played again for 14 years.

1942

The Rose Bowl game is moved to Duke University in North Carolina because of World War II attack threats.

1947

The Rose Bowl sells out its tickets for the first time and every year after.

1952

The Rose Bowl is the first college football game to be broadcast nationally on television.

1953

The Rose Bowl Player of the Game Award is created.

1973

A record crowd of 106,869 people attend the Rose Bowl.

1989

The Rose Bowl celebrates its 75th anniversary.

1998

The Rose Bowl becomes part of the Bowl Championship Series.

2010

The Rose Bowl hosts two post-season football games. Ohio State defeats Oregon 26–17 to win the Rose Bowl. One week later, Alabama defeats Texas 37–21 to win the BCS national championship.

QUICK FACTS

- The Rose Bowl has showcased 17 Heisman Memorial Trophy winners. This trophy is given to the Most Outstanding College Football player.

- The Rose Bowl has honored 104 college football legends, inducting them into the Rose Bowl Hall of Fame.

Test Your Knowledge

1 What year was the first Rose Bowl game played?

2 How long does it take to play a football game?

3 How many players are on the field at one time for a team?

4 What position is responsible for throwing or running with the ball when the play starts?

5 What is the highest attendance at a Rose Bowl game?

6 What Rose Bowl legend has the award for the best linebacker in college football named after him?

7 What city does the Tournament of Roses take place in?

8 What was the one year that the Rose Bowl did not take place in California?

9 What is the name of the first stadium in Pasadena that was used for the Rose Bowl?

10 Who was the last player to win the Rose Bowl MVP award two years in a row?

ANSWERS: 1.) 1902 2.) There are four quarters in a game of football. Each quarter is 15 minutes in length. It takes about three hours to play four 15-minute quarters. 3.) Eleven players 4.) Quarterback 5.) 106,869 people in 1973 6.) Dick Butkus 7.) Pasadena, California 8.) 1942 9.) Tournament Park 10.) Vince Young

Key Words

amateur: a person who is not paid to play a sport

bowl game: a post-season college football game

conference: a group of teams

defensive: the team that is trying to keep the opposition from scoring on their end of the field

flag football: a type of football where players have a flag pulled from their uniform instead of being tackled

foul: an unfair act

kick return: to catch a ball from a kickoff and run it in the opposite direction

offensive: the team that has the ball and is attempting to score

pass completion: a successful forward pass

punter: a player who drops the ball from his or her hands and kicks it before it touches the ground

retroactively: to take effect from a date in the past

semi-professional: to play a sport for money but not as a full-time career

snap: putting the football into play by throwing the football between the player's legs, backwards from the line of scrimmage to the quarterback or another player

spectators: people who are watching an event take place live

touch football: a type of football where players are touched to stop the play, instead of tackled

turf: a layer of matted earth, held together by grass and grass roots; artificial turf is synthetic or carpet-like materials made to look like grass, used as a surface for football fields

underdog: the team that is expected to lose the game

uprights: posts that extend upright from the back of the end zone

Index

Log on to www.av2books.com

AV² by Weigl brings you media enhanced books that support active learning. Go to www.av2books.com, and enter the special code found on page 2 of this book. You will gain access to enriched and enhanced content that supplements and complements this book. Content includes video, audio, weblinks, quizzes, a slide show, and activities.

AV² Online Navigation

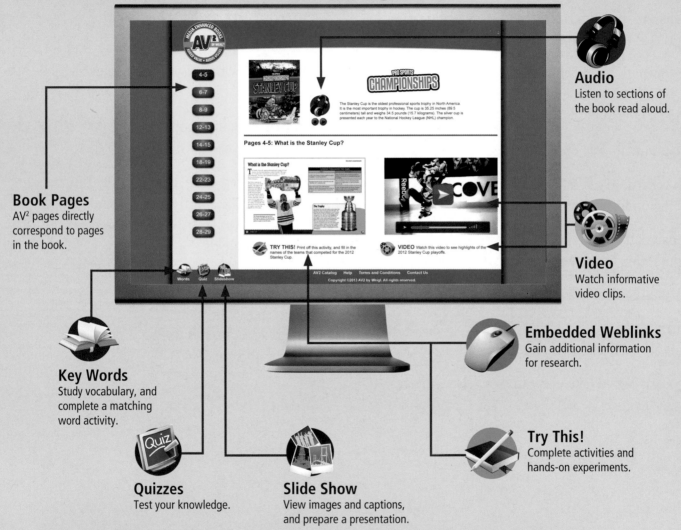

Audio
Listen to sections of the book read aloud.

Book Pages
AV² pages directly correspond to pages in the book.

Video
Watch informative video clips.

Key Words
Study vocabulary, and complete a matching word activity.

Embedded Weblinks
Gain additional information for research.

Try This!
Complete activities and hands-on experiments.

Quizzes
Test your knowledge.

Slide Show
View images and captions, and prepare a presentation.

AV² was built to bridge the gap between print and digital. We encourage you to tell us what you like and what you want to see in the future.

Sign up to be an AV² Ambassador at www.av2books.com/ambassador.

Due to the dynamic nature of the Internet, some of the URLs and activities provided as part of AV² by Weigl may have changed or ceased to exist. AV² by Weigl accepts no responsibility for any such changes. All media enhanced books are regularly monitored to update addresses and sites in a timely manner. Contact AV² by Weigl at 1-866-649-3445 or av2books@weigl.com with any questions, comments, or feedback.